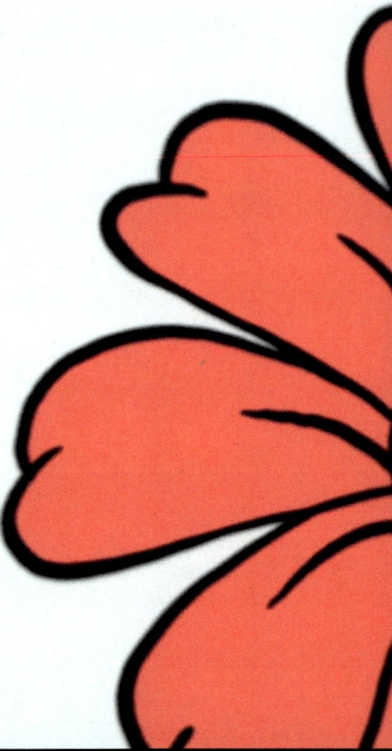

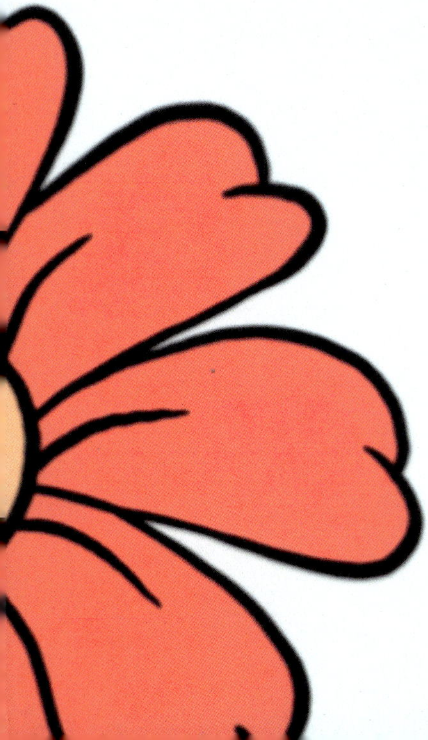

This Book Belongs To:
_____

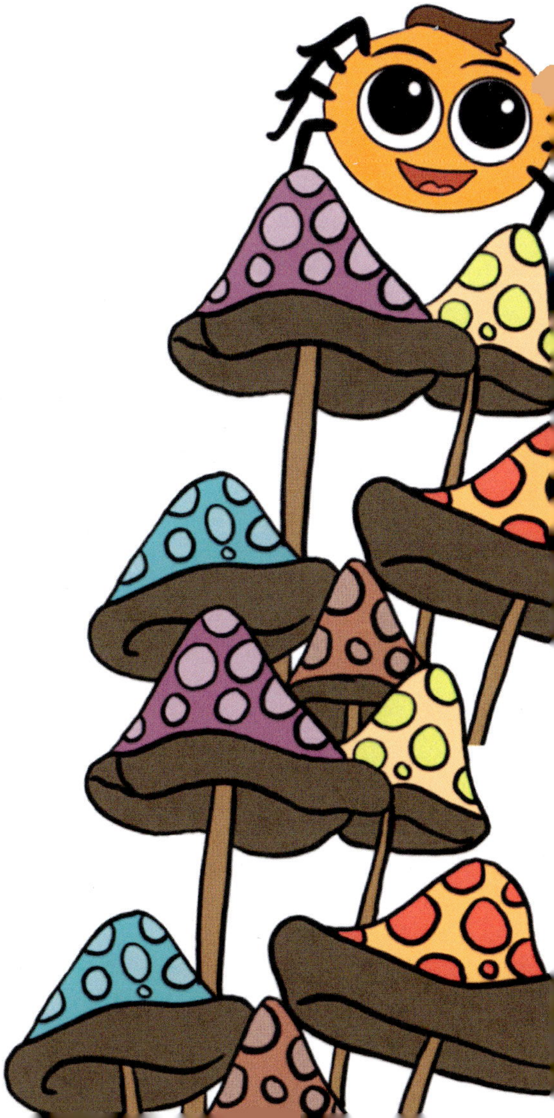

This book is dedicated to my

Heavenly Father who gifted me with persistence and faith, to develop this science literature. To my most loving, giving and supportive mom who is the wind beneath my wings; and to my beautiful and devoted daughter who serves as a constant reflection of my purpose.

The Itsy Bitsy Water Cycle

How many legs does my friend Itsy Bitsy have to climb the water spout?

The Itsy Bitsy spider
climbed up the water spout

Clouds condensed...

What state of matter do water molecules change to when condensed to clouds?

What are the four forms of precipitation?

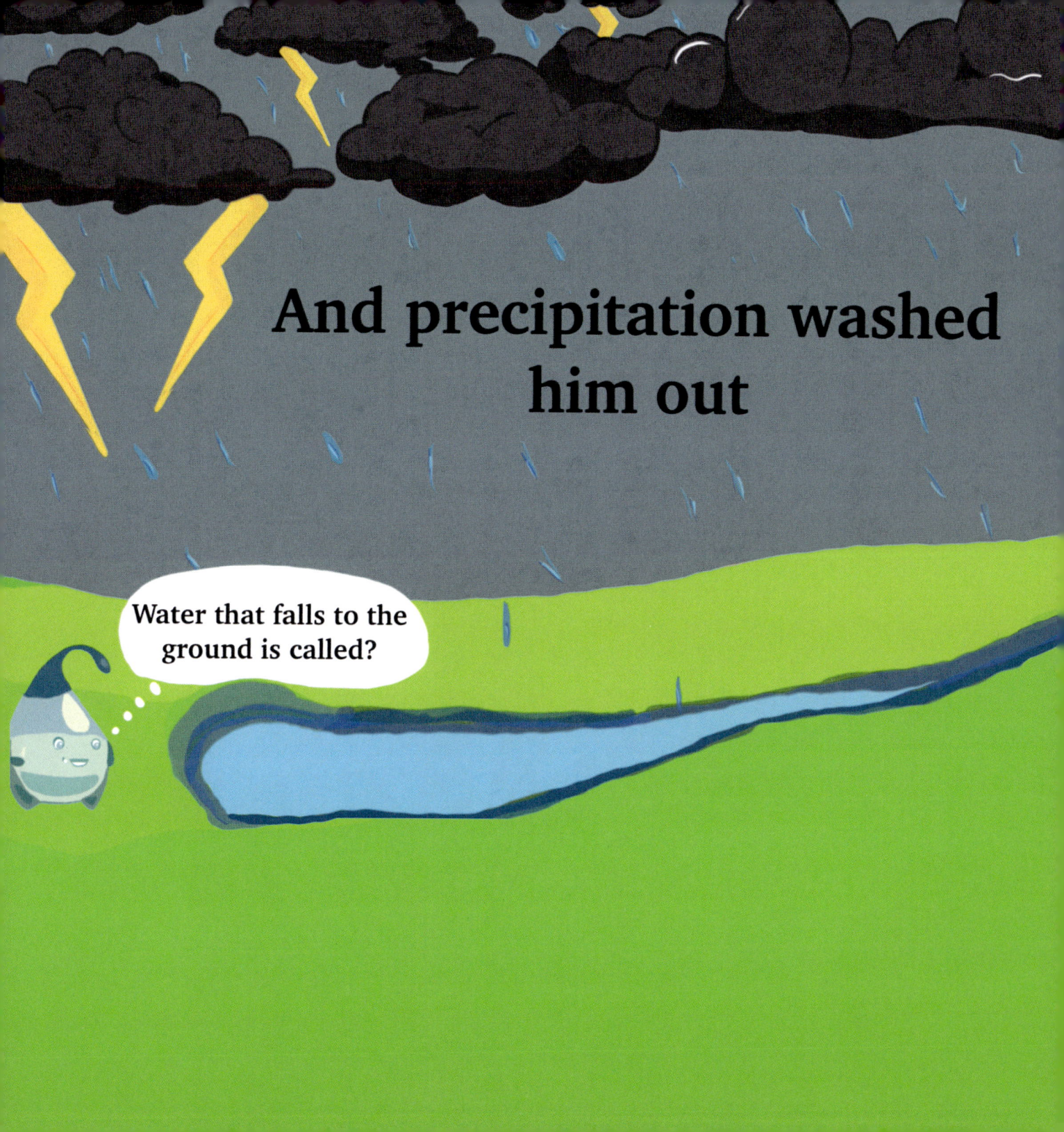

And precipitation washed him out

Water that falls to the ground is called?

Out came the solar energy

What are three ways the Sun helps Earth?

Could the water cycle exist without the Sun?
Why or Why not?

And evaporated all the rain.

What state of matter do water molecules change to when evaporated?

And the Itsy Bitsy spider,

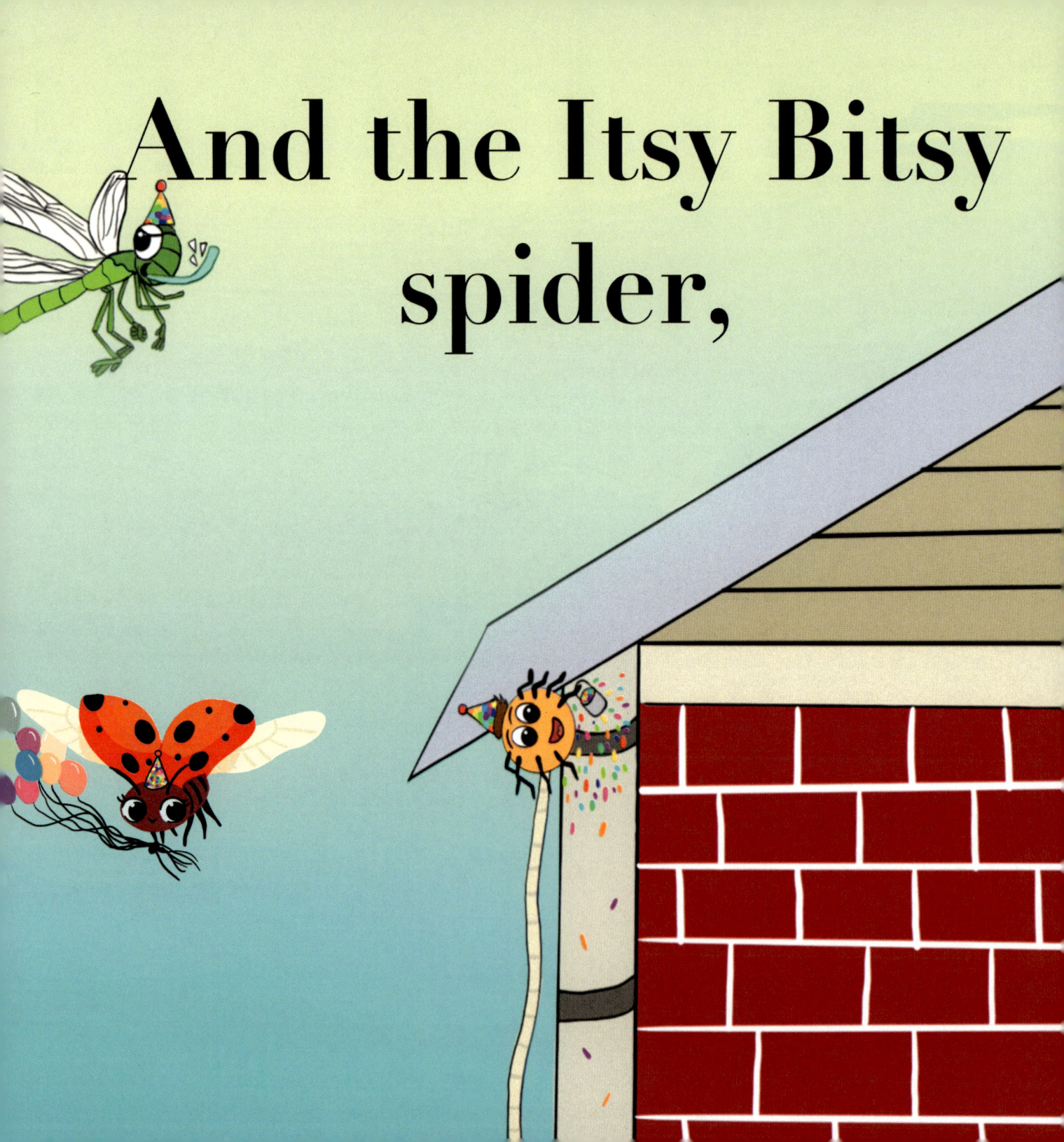

Climbed up the water Spout again.

What are three processes that make up the water cycle?

QUESTION & ANSWERS

Q1. How many legs do spiders have to climb up & down?

Q2. What state of matter do water molecules change to when condensed?

Q3. Water that falls to the ground is called?

Q4. What are four forms of precipitation?

QUESTION & ANSWERS

A1. Spiders have eight legs. Spiders are known as Arachnids not Insects. They belong to the largest group of animals on Earth called Arthropods.

A2. Water molecules change from a state of gas to liquid when they are condensed. As water molecules (water vapor) rise in the air they become cool and form clouds. Fog is another form of condensation.

A3. Precipitation: Water molecules become too heavy in the clouds and fall to the Earth.

A4. Rain, Snow, Sleet or Hail are at least four forms of precipitation.

QUESTION & ANSWERS

Q5. Could the water cycle exist without the Sun? Why or Why Not?

Q6. What are three ways the Sun helps Earth?

Q7. What state of matter do water molecules change to when evaporated?

Q8. What are three processes that make up the water cycle?

QUESTION & ANSWERS

A5. No, the sun gives off heat which warms the Earth. As a result the process of evaporation, condensation, and precipitation creates a cycle that repeats itself.

A6.
1) Gives Earth light
2) Warms the land
3) Triggers plant photosynthesis (Helps grow fruit and vegetables)

A7. Water molecules change from a state of liquid to gas when they are evaporated. The water molecules then start to move faster in this process.

A8. Evaporation, Condensation, and Precipitation:
Evaporation- Surface water becomes water vapor (gas). Condensation- When water vapor turns to liquid and helps form clouds. Precipitation- Liquid that falls to the ground.

The Itsy Bitsy Water Cycle

Condensation

Precipitation

Evaporation

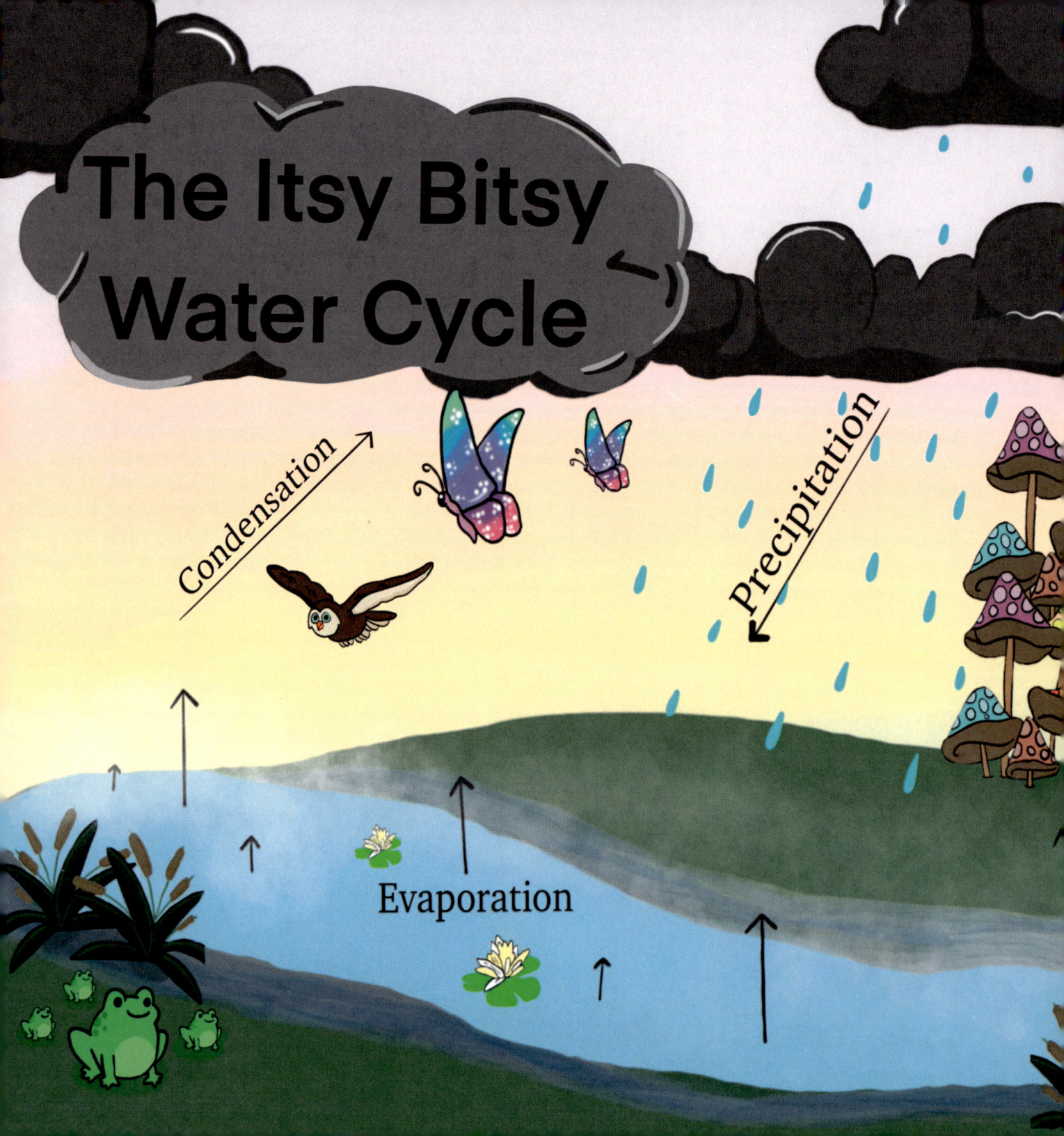

About the illustrator

Emma Johnson is an entrepreneur, activist, and educator who loves to help others. She has had a passion for inspiring the next generation for as long as she can remember. As of 2021 Emma has started her journey to become a Early Childhood- 6th grade Educator that is certified in Special Populations and ESL. Emma became inspired to start writing and illustrating books because she saw a educational need around the world to bring science literature to life for all students.

Emma is not done living her dream yet. She wants to help become a voice for the voiceless and a face for the faceless.

Made in the USA
Columbia, SC
10 November 2022